SIMPLE FENG SHUI

Gina Lazenby

WATSON-GUPTILL Publications/New York

Text copyright © Gina Lazenby 2000
Design and layout copyright ©
Conran Octopus 1999
Artwork copyright © Conran Octopus 1999

First published in the United States in 2000
by Watson-Guptill Publications,
a division of BPI Communications. Inc.,
770 Broadway, New York, NY 10003

COMMISSIONING EDITOR:Kate Bell
PROJECT EDITOR:Sarah Sears
EDITORIAL ASSISTANT:Alexandra Kent
ART EDITOR:Mary Staples
PICTURE RESEARCH: Jessica Walton,
Mel Watson
PRODUCTION: Oliver Jeffreys

Library of Congress Catalog Card Number:
99-67568

ISBN 0-8230-4835-7

First published in the United Kingdom in
1999 by Conran Octopus Limited,
2–4 Heron Quays, London E14 4JP

Colour origination by Sang Choy
International, Singapore.

Printed in China

First printing 1999

2 3 4 5 6 7 8 9 / 07 06 05 04 03 02 01 00

contents

WHAT IS FENG SHUI?

The simplest way to understand feng shui is to think of it as our intuitive response to a space. We all know what it is like when we decide to move house and visit other homes that are for sale. Some of the properties just do not feel right to us – they have 'bad vibes' – while others feel more welcoming and comfortable and just seem to 'click'. What is it about a building or home that can have such an effect? Aspects of architecture and construction have been combined with traditional notions of room usage, as well as fashionable interior design dictates concerning colour, texture, light, patterns and sound, to create a certain vitality in a space. This can perhaps best be understood if we think of everything as being made up of energy as defined by quantum physics: everything in the universe is simply energy vibrating at different frequencies – some you can see and some you cannot. Energy, or chi, moves around our homes like an invisible breath, and what the study of feng shui seeks to do is ensure that this energy is of a consistently high quality and kept moving at a healthy pace.

Deep within ourselves we know what suits our personal needs. If we let go and gave free rein to our intuition we would probably make much healthier choices for our homes. We know exactly the best place to sit or eat, the interior design scheme and

colours that will relax us, and the shapes that will help us become alert and focused. There is something about the man-made nature of our environments and the fast pace of our lives that separates us from that little voice of inner wisdom. We forget what we already know. This book will help to find that voice again.

Now, as our homes become even more important to us as retreats and oases of calm, safe from what some people feel is an increasingly aggressive outside world, we are

Long, low, soft-cushioned seating creates a relaxing and comfortable antidote here to the hard stone floor. The big windows let in a lot of light and summer heat but blue and lavender tones keep the room cool. The light walls, natural materials and straight lines combine to create an oasis of calm.

being drawn to find out more about how previous generations and other traditional cultures arranged their lives. We have much to learn from ancient wisdom, which is why feng shui, developed over the centuries in the Far East, has become so popular.

It seems that the antidote to a complex and stressful world is to live a more simple life. Feng shui can help you to achieve this. There is no need to embrace Oriental interior design just because feng shui originated in China; all you need to do is connect with a few simple universal principles.

What you have to do is ensure that the invisible energy or chi can move freely and unobstructed through your home. For if anything gets in the way of that easy flow, it will also get between you and an easy life: stuff … clutter … obstructions. The new mantra seems to be 'Get rid of what you don't need and keep what you love.' As you throw things away, you will create space, increasing the chances of attracting things to yourself that you really desire or feel you need. Use this book to give yourself some simple guidelines for creating a home environment that will help to de-stress you.

THE BAGUA
AND YOUR HOME

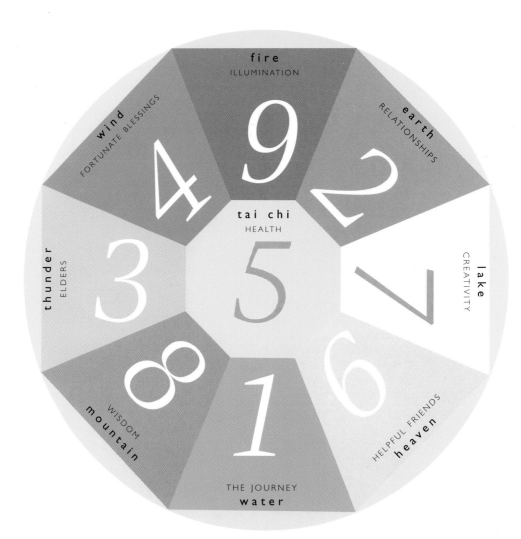

fire
ILLUMINATION

earth
RELATIONSHIPS

wind
FORTUNATE BLESSINGS

tai chi
HEALTH

lake
CREATIVITY

thunder
ELDERS

WISDOM
mountain

HELPFUL FRIENDS
heaven

THE JOURNEY
water

WHAT IS THE BAGUA?

Your hallway is important as it creates a first impression of your home. It should be clear of clutter, and a bright flower arrangement here will stimulate the energy passing through into the house.

Throughout history peoples from all over the world have studied man's position between earth and heaven – and the nature of the relationship it formed. As they studied the cycles of the seasons and the movement of the planets and were guided by their observations of the natural world, they came to understand the way in which different homes could affect their well-being and good fortune in life.

Feng shui has been practised in the East for thousands of years. Over time, different forms developed as practitioners classified in various maps and tables how they understood the nature of the world, and worked out different systems for looking at the movement of energy. The bagua is one such energy map which, along with an understanding of the importance of symbolism, will help you to work intuitively to improve your relationship with your home.

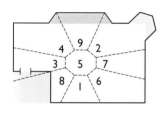

Your home is another layer of yourself, a mirror of your life, reflecting what is going on for you at many different levels. Physical clutter mirrors chaotic thinking, while someone's collection of pictures of solitary people can correspond with a lack of a satisfying relationship. You can employ the principles of feng shui in your home to support you in your quest for a new way of being, for by making feng shui placements you will be giving yourself physical reminders of what you want.

If you want to change your life, the first thing you have to do is decide how you want the future to be. Who are you hoping to attract; what new event, situation or circumstance are you hoping to prompt? When, finally, you feel you know clearly what you want, then you can focus on it. It is at this stage that you should give some signal to your unconscious that you mean business, by making a change, however minor, in your physical environment.

The top diagram shows a negative space in 4 Wind, which might relate to a lack of money or opportunity, but which can be counterbalanced by stimulating the flow of chi in that area. The diagram below it has extensions in 2 Earth and 9 Fire as well as a negative space in 8 Wisdom. You can make adjustments to energize these negative spaces outside as well as in the house itself.

The ancient bagua, an energy map which describes the way energy moves in a predictable pattern within a defined space, will help you both to reveal your current situation and to identify what adjustments you should make to improve it.

The bagua (see page 10) is a flexible template divided into nine areas, which you lay over a plan of your property or land, your house, apartment – even a room; you can stretch it to fit over any shape.

Each of the nine 'houses' relates to a certain set of characteristics. When, for example, energy is moving

invisibly in the area of the bagua known as 2 Earth, it will have some sort of impact on a relationship issue in the physical world. Similarly, if there is any disturbance to the flow of energy in the area of 4 Wind, the fortune or finances of the house's occupants are likely to be adversely affected.

Always orient the bagua from the front door of your home or main doorway into a room. Align your stretched grid of nine numbers with your floorplan so that your door opens somewhere along the side consisting of the numbers

Careful placement of bright objects – those that glint and sparkle as well as the more obvious mirrors and glasses – will enhance the level of energy in a dark corner, and by increasing the energy in a particular house of the bagua, you will encourage change in the part of your life corresponding to that space.

8, 1 and 6. If the area in question has more than one entrance, use the main one; if you use your front door only rarely and generally use the back door instead, you should still orient the bagua on the front door.

Although the bagua for the ground floor floorplan of a building is the most powerful, each storey will have its own bagua: use the top step onto the landing as the 'front door'. Remember, too, that you can apply the bagua to individual rooms, and that doorways can be open entrances without solid doors. Sometimes a room will be a 'crossroads' with three or four doorways: always line up the bagua's 8, 1, 6 side with the wall broken by the doorway most frequently used.

Your home may be irregularly shaped, and you may find that it contains 'negative spaces' or 'extensions'. Generally, if the extension forms more than half of the area from where it protrudes, then it leaves a negative space; less than half, it is an extension (see diagrams on page12), which means that the prevailing energy of that house will be greater. Irregularly shaped houses should not be seen as a bad thing; rather, with the adjustments you can make in each of the nine houses, their potential to offer you new possibilities is tremendous.

NEGATIVE SPACE

• Don't be alarmed when you discover a 'negative space'; while it may create a depletion of energy for a particular house of the bagua, there are a few simple additions that will address the imbalance, regardless of which sector of the bagua is missing.

• Place a mirror on the wall next to the negative space so that when you look at the wall the mirror creates the illusion that there is something going on behind it.

• A painting with a long depth of field – a long, straight French road with an avenue of trees, for example – pulls your own energy and attention into it.

• Crystals expand the energy that comes in from the light outside and will magnify the energy of any house of the bagua whether it is missing or simply needs a boost, so hang a small, round, faceted crystal in a window bounding a negative space, so that it showers the room with coloured rainbows when the sun shines.

• If you have access to the space outside on the ground floor, square up the plot and place a light in the corner that would have been the corner of the building. Bringing plants and garden decorations into this enclosure will further boost the energy.

water
T H E   J O U R N E Y

The first house of the bagua is Water. It represents not only the job you have now and your career, but also your journey through life. Many people ask 'Why am I here?' 'What is it all for?' If you are not doing what you want to do, and do not find your life fulfilling, look hard at this part of your home. The sector includes your front door or the area next to it. If your home physically lacks this area, you are likely to be finding it difficult to get onto your path or find a job; a projection here, meanwhile, will generate extra energy which could help you to discover what it is you really do want to do and your career will shine. The entrance must be uncluttered – blockages here will impede your progress in life.

• Associated with the direction of north, the season of winter and the time of midnight, Water is nourished by the colours blue and black and any images of water.

• Boost the energy by introducing the water element with a fishtank or representations of moving water– or with flowing lines. Avoid still water, which leads to stagnation.

• Choose your pictures carefully: either those that represent what you want to do or, if you have no idea yet, look for pictures depicting roads or routes, or historical maps – symbols to help you find your way.

earth
RELATIONSHIPS
2

The Earth sector is about receptivity and openness, reinforced by soft things and low shapes. Energy here is manifested in the physical world in relationships; it is often called the marriage corner. A woman might find it difficult to live in a house where this sector is missing because the shortfall in energy is in the most feminine area of the house. It is likely too that a couple living there might be experiencing problems and it could be the reason why a single occupant is still single. To maintain harmony, you must ensure that none of your home's relationship corners is a negative space, and that they are all as clutter-free as possible: the bedroom, where you are closest to yourself and your partner, is the most crucial.

• The direction is here is south-west, the season late summer and the time late afternoon.

• Boost a negative space or enhance a relationship by introducing a mirror, ceramic containers, soft cushions, candlepower, yellows and brown tones and a touch of red for passion.

• Keep this corner sweet and soft. Bring nature into the environment with flowers, plants and water, but avoid harsh symbols, like cacti.

• Replace images of solitary figures with pictures of couples having fun or even pairs of swans or flowers – images of partnership and unity.

thunder 3
ELDERS

The third house of the bagua is associated with the family, our Elders. It represents our entire past. Thus it is the ideal place to express gratitude to our family, for no words need to be spoken. It is also the sector that will influence our ability to get new projects started. It signifies vitality, movement and new beginnings. Sometimes when you have family rifts that remain unresolved, they can somehow hold you back from creating the future that you really want, so you need to work in this area if you want to stimulate some gentle healing. A projection here will mean a great sense of maturity in the household but if this section is missing, occupants will lack energy and endurance, and may have family problems.

• The direction is east, the season is spring and the time of day is sunrise.

• If the area is missing, put a mirror on an interior wall for an illusion of space and introduce some green.

• Artwork characterized by upward movement or images featuring woodlands or tall items, like columns and tall furniture, are good symbols; they will help to stimulate a new enterprise and family harmony.

• Displays of happy family photographs of your parents and grandparents will be ideal here, alongside treasured mementoes.

• Have a clear out: holding onto useless things from the past can symbolize an inability or an unwillingness to move forward.

wind 4
FORTUNATE BLESSINGS

Wind corresponds with good fortune. The image here is of a flexible tree that bends in the wind. It represents growth, maturing, and ideas brought to you like seeds on the winds of change. Although the energy here does manifest itself in the world as money, which explains why this house is often referred to as the 'wealth corner', many of life's real blessings will, in fact, come to you in currency other than money: opportunities, invitations, your children and friends. When a house lacks this area, the chances that you will suffer a misfortune or accident are increased. If there is a projection on a home here, the household will prosper and everything the occupants put their energy into tends to be successful.

• The direction associated with Wind is north-west and the season late spring.

• A small cut-glass crystal hung in a window here will certainly boost the energy of good fortune in this sector. Mobiles, fans and moving sculptures all stimulate the energy of Wind and thus will boost this sector.

• Choose adjustments that are characterized by wood energy: plants and the colours green and blue. Because wood likes to be nourished by water this is also an ideal situation for an indoor fountain or fishtank.

• If a negative space in this sector is occupied outside by a part of your garden, invest in exterior lighting, a bird bath and attractive plantings; they will still generate positive energy and activate the space, even if outside.

tai chi 5
HEALTH

Five is in the centre of the bagua and represents a unifying of all forces. It is an important meeting point for all the energies, so the Tai Chi is an important point of stability and balance. Whatever is happening here will affect the stability of your life, family, health, relationships and all your projects, because this house contains aspects of all the areas. Ancient cultures would often leave an open courtyard in the centre of their house and, indeed, if this area is missing in your home, it will be a bonus; keeping the central core of your home clear will promote the free flow of energy. Keep the middle of each room empty, particularly the living room – an important social gathering point towards which people tend to gravitate.

• Although it has no compass direction, the Tai Chi is strongly associated with the earth energy in 2 Earth and 8 Mountain.

• Real vitality and well-being can only be achieved if everything is in balance, and as this area is most important for your health, it is vital to keep it clean, tidy and uncluttered.

• Reinforce the connection with Earth by making the space feel harmonious with ceramics, anything soft and receptive, or empty containers. These will remind you to stay centred and grounded, thereby strengthening your life.

heaven 6
HELPFUL FRIENDS

Heaven represents the creative force of the universe and the source of all things. It is associated with the archetype of the father, with authority, strength and leadership, and affects your ability both to complete projects and create tangible rewards – like cashflow. This house is also known as Helpful Friends, it represents all your visible and invisible means of support, as well as the spirit of philanthropy and your willingness to give of yourself to others. A negative space in this area may mean that you lack the support of friends, and experience difficulty with authority or with male superiors at work; men may feel undermined. Meanwhile, a projection in this area will lead to a sociable household, but women may feel less comfortable.

• Associated with the direction of north-west, the phase of late autumn, and the colours white and silver, Heaven can be represented by jewels, precious stones, crystals, symbols of authority, legends and myths.

• Stimulate this corner with curved shapes and bowls, particularly those made of metal.

• If you are looking for a more active social life, this is the ideal place for your address book; and if you feel in need of support, pictures of angels here will help.

• If your built-in garage occupies this house, you will need to counteract the negative effects with plants and lighting.

• Become a helpful person – do some voluntary work or make charitable donations – and you will stimulate the energy in your home too.

lake 7
CREATIVITY

The nature of Lake is like the youngest daughter in a family – free-spirited and full of hope and joy. It represents your senses, an appreciation of the arts, and pleasure. This house relates to your imagination and your ability to create in any area – be it the everyday household routines, poetry, or having children, the ultimate act of creation. If there is a projection in this part of a house, a sociable household that makes things materialize will probably be living there; if the area is lacking, pleasure will be lacking too, and creativity (and fertility) will be a problem. If the space is just too full and overcrowded, creativity can become stifled – just as our ability to think is thwarted by an overloaded mind.

• Lake energy is synonymous with the late-afternoon sunsets of the west, the season of autumn, the golden glow in the sky, romance, and harvest time, when things are brought to fruition.

• Anything which gives you pleasure – from ornaments and photographs to games and prized possessions – carries the essence of Lake and would sit well in this sector.

• Associated with metal, Lake can be stimulated by white and gold colours, metal objects, images of lakes and symbols of what we want to create or what inspires us.

• If the Lake area is too full it will reflect an overloaded mind. Empty your head of old ideas and clear out the clutter from your home in order to allow new creative energy to flourish.

mountain 8
WISDOM

Mountain is about contemplation and inner knowledge, and like the cave within the mountain, you need to be empty to be receptive to wisdom rather than simply being filled with knowledge. Qualities include heaviness, solidity, quiet and inertia, which relate not only to a great strength of will, new beginnings, being single-minded and putting effort into achieving, but also to the struggle to become established. The inner calm of Mountain can affect your relationships with others too. If your home lacks this corner, it will be difficult to feel peaceful and secure, and new beginnings are more difficult from a base of instability. But a projection here should be avoided too: this house needs symmetry.

•The direction is north-east, the time is that period just before dawn and just before Spring.

•Containers like vases and heavy furniture like chests and cupboards carry the nature of Mountain.

•Choose a mountain sector somewhere in your home to create a quiet corner for contemplation and meditation; a bedroom in this sector of your home will feel quiet.

• Boost your sense of self by nourishing Mountain with symbols of fire energy – red, triangles and light.

• Counteract a projection in Mountain with metal objects, the colour white and curved shapes.

fire
ILLUMINATION
9

The true essence of Fire is about clarity, vision, visibility and the eye, understanding and enlightenment, and relates to the self and others. Its nature is expressed in light, candles and anything created from inspiration or likely to inspire you – like sculpture, poetry, ceremonies and rituals, art by the great masters, classical music, treasures and sacred objects. If this area of your house is missing, eyesight might be a physical problem, alongside an emotional lack of illumination and clarity, and problems with getting well known. A projection will be beneficial in terms of fame and recognition, but, given Fire's explosive and unpredictable nature, this may become notoriety; it could be dark secrets that come to light.

• The direction is the south, symbolic shapes are flame-like and triangular, and the colour is red.

• The energy of Fire radiates in all directions and is like the peak of activity in the midday sun in summer.

• If you are not feeling inspired, you may be lacking Fire around you. Stimulate a negative space in this area with art, a mirror on the wall, lights, and flame-like colours and shapes.

• Illumination is synonymous with finding your way; you may have to introduce extra lighting if you are looking for clarity.

FENG SHUI
IN PRACTICE

ENTRANCES & HALLS

Often paid too little attention, entrances are, in fact, very important, for they signify how we relate to society. Giving strong messages to the outside world about who we are and acting as the vital link between this and the inner world of our home, they should be as welcoming as possible and free of obstruction to ease the flow of energy, people, opportunities and resources into our lives.

◀ *Entrances are the gateways of chi, or energy, into the home. So the more difficult it is for people to find your door, the more difficult it is for opportunity to knock on it. Make your door visible, particularly if it is hidden from the road or at the side of the house. Make sure that it is clearly demarcated and well lit. Symmetrical plantings, ornamental door guardians or statues are best, as they will uplift people's spirits every time they pass, but a boot scraper will also define an entrance.*

Ensure that you install good outside lighting; check that your doorbell works, and that the door opens easily and fully. If you do not change burned out lightbulbs promptly, you may feel unclear about your sense of direction, and if you have to push a door that is warped or that catches on the mat, the path of your own life may not be smooth. Fixing a broken doorbell, however, may be enough to prompt a job offer or a more active social life.

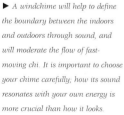

▶ *A windchime will help to define the boundary between the indoors and outdoors through sound, and will moderate the flow of fast-moving chi. It is important to choose your chime carefully; how its sound resonates with your own energy is more crucial than how it looks.*

Hallways should feel open and receptive too, for what people see as soon as they go through the front door will affect their experience of the house as a whole. So, if your entrance or hallway is small and narrow, or opens straight onto a wall, it is important that the area is bright and clear.

◀ *Hallways act as a transitional space and should be free of distracting objects, in order to make the migration from the exterior to the interior world as smooth as possible.*

▶ *Staircases are important for aiding the flow of chi around a home. The inviting curve of this staircase encourages that flow and is most impressive. As it sweeps upwards we cannot see where it will end, which is symbolic of our future; we might know the general direction but we cannot know for sure what that future will be.*

tips for entrances & halls

• Set the mood in the hall for how you will experience the rest of the house. Use mirrors, lighting, artwork and flowers to keep the energy here welcoming and bright, reflecting your hospitality.

• Shiny door fittings encourage more chi into the home and protect you if a road runs straight up to your home.

• Chi must be slowed down in long halls and corridors. If you can see right through the house from the front door, break up the view with a windchime, rounded plant containers, or artwork and half-moon shelves.

• If several doors lead off the hall, keep open only the one leading into the main welcoming area – probably the living room.

• Chi should not be given easy ways to escape from the home: rounded stairs, or a mirror or shiny object behind the front door, will turn the energy back inside.

• Leave shoes in the hall, keeping the energy of the outside world away from your sanctuary.

In order to achieve the maximum flow of energy, it is essential to keep hallways and corridors clear of clutter and obstructions; indeed you should avoid overwhelming your visitors with too busy a decorative scheme or complicated artwork on the walls. The beautiful curved wall here (above) provides a smooth passageway for the energy. A potentially stark area, it is made more welcoming by the plant that stands on the small, round table.

You don't get to choose how you are going to die. Or when.
You can only decide how you are going to live. Now.

JOAN BAEZ

LIVING ROOMS

Today's living rooms are multi-functional rooms; they are the most public area of the home, where we receive visitors, and also a private space, where we can settle and relax – by watching television, talking or reading. It is important that the space suits both uses; it should be welcoming and comfortable. Try to hide your television otherwise it will attract your attention and get turned on too often.

The living room is where you should display your art collections and precious antiques, but be aware that whatever you choose gives clues to visitors about your personality and aspirations. Make sure too that you choose well, that you really like the pieces you display because you will have to look at them every day.

Position your furniture so that there is an easy flow of energy around the room; avoid clutter and too many tables. This is the main gathering room and the hub of family life, where you live together and where your friends should feel entirely at ease. It is in this room that energy will collect before it disperses around the rest of the house and through the family.

In a room where your sofa is placed in the centre, so that your back is to the door and you cannot see who is coming in, you need to create some kind of supporting structure behind you. A table here offers protection to people as they sit on the sofa facing into the room.

▶ *Light is energy. You can make
dramatic changes to the mood and
feel of a room by turning off a bright
central light and switching on
smaller lamps to illuminate dark
corners and create low pools of light.
By introducing light fixtures in
appropriate places in a room, you
can also activate particular areas
of the bagua. A lamp is usually a
good correction for negative space in
a particular house of the bagua.*

▼ *Different shapes have different energies that will affect an area: whereas curves are linked with creativity, squares represent organization and rational thinking. Try to bring a balance of both into a room. The softer and more free-flowing the shapes, the more relaxing a room will be. Where possible, choose furniture which has rounded corners and edges.*

◀ *It is helpful to be able to alter the amount of bright light in a room, because the energy requirements of a living room vary according to its different roles. The combination of blinds and sheer curtains here provide just such flexibility as regards light, as well as being an attractive window dressing – the fringed swag softening an otherwise rather hard-edged treatment. If you do not have a fireplace, arrange the seating around a central table like this, softened and brightened by a large display of flowers.*

▶ *A fireplace usually creates the ideal focal point in a room, and its warmth is very welcoming. The placement of a mirror over a fireplace emphasizes that focal point, while the reflective silver surface of the mirror also provides a cooling antidote to the heat of the fire. Be very conscious of what the mirror is reflecting: if your room is cluttered a mirror will extend the confusion and whatever difficulties you have will effectively be doubled.*

tips for living rooms

- Hang pictures of places you would like to visit in the future, not just those you have loved in the past.

- Fresh flowers keep energy refreshed; dried flowers hold stagnation and should be changed seasonally.

- Do not overfill the room with furniture; ensure you leave enough space for people to congregate.

- Avoid glass-topped tables: you cannot relax fully around a hard, sharp edge.

- If you have ceiling beams, do not place a seat directly underneath them. Anyone sitting there regularly may begin to suffer from headaches.

- Position chairs so that they do not face a sharp angle or square corner; the energy here can be very uncomfortable.

- Don't let the television dominate the room – make a clear distinction between the focal point of the room and the television.

▼ *Research shows that the creation of a mood in a room is more important than arranging the space simply for its function. Today, living rooms are seen as needing to be places to get together as a family, corners for stimulating conversation and areas where we can retreat to wind down and relax – all at the same time. Colour is a very powerful tool and can have as much effect on the nature of a room as the shape of the furniture and its arrangement. The yellow tones here have a gathering effect and make the room cheerful.*

▶ *Our homes are full of symbols which are constantly affecting our energy. The art we hang on our walls can be a potent source of inspiration: displays of pictures of your family – photographs or paintings – will reinforce a sense of cohesion in the household. If we focus on something, it will attract energy and it will become a catalyst, starting to draw in the events and people which are necessary to make things happen in our lives. Conversely, on a negative note, you may find that if you surround yourself with stark landscape paintings populated only by solitary figures, you may feel lonely. Similarly, hanging abstract art on your walls when you want clarity and focus could well leave you feeling fragmented and incomplete.*

◄ *Conservatories can be difficult rooms in which to relax because so much energy drains away through the large expanses of glass. Here the magnificent plants hold the focus in the room. In smaller rooms it is still worth having plants on the windowsill to bring your focus back into the room, otherwise your valuable energy will be dispersed unnecessarily. Moreover, plants by windows also act as powerful, natural protection against noise and air pollution.*

► *It is best not to have any seat with its back to the door, and very important to make sure that the host's chair is in a commanding position – ideally facing the door and with the protection of a wall behind it. Clusters of chairs arranged to face a television will let the television dominate the room, making communication difficult. Arranging chairs around a hearth or coffee table is infinitely preferable.*

The secret of life is balance, and the absence of balance is life's destruction.

HAZRAT INAYAT KHAN

KITCHENS/DINING ROOMS

Our personal energy levels are dependent upon our ability to absorb nutrients from food, and this will be severely diminished if the kitchen environment is chaotic and untidy. Instead, to encourage a steady flow of chi, it must be clean, orderly and free from clutter, and there should be plenty of space and good organization and storage.

The roles of both the kitchen and the dining room are crucial for creating and maintaining our good health, because the food we cook and eat generates new life within us. The kitchen forms the very heart of the home. It is also the most important room as regards our nourishment – both physical and spiritual – so it is vital that the person who carries out the cooking in the house does so in a calm atmosphere with the minimum disturbance. Any jarring interruptions will affect the cook's energy. Thus, you should ensure that food preparation areas are not situated in corners that are exposed to the negative force of a sharp angle or shelf. Avoid having the kitchen as a walk-through so that when you are cooking you are not constantly disturbed by other people's activity directly in your pathway.

Where the kitchen is situated in the home has a bearing on family life. If the kitchen appears to be 'outside' the building, protruding from the front door as an extension, then the occupants are likely to eat out often. If it is clearly visible from the front door, or indeed, if you walk straight into the kitchen when you enter the house, then food will be your focus whenever you arrive home.

◀ *Ideally, you will cook and eat in separate rooms, but if you have to use the kitchen as a dining room, make sure that you clear away your utensils and draw attention away from all the preparatory functions before you start to eat, either by screening off the kitchen area or by dimming the lighting. Use candles or put a good light above the dining table, rather than having a bright general light in the room.*

▼ *The kitchen controls the pulse of the home. If this room is characterized by simplicity and clear organization, these qualities will pervade both the food preparation and the occupants of the household alike. Clean, orderly storage of kitchen equipment – particularly important in kitchens with open shelving – not only ensures that calmness will be the order of the day but inspires the cook to create delicious meals too. Despite the attractive orderliness here, it is always preferable to store sharp knives out of sight.*

◄ *It is best to eat in a comfortable place in an unhurried atmosphere. Avoid being overly distracted by stimulating pictures on the walls, or clutter and mess on the table. Whatever you can introduce in the way of natural objects and materials will make your space more cosy and relaxing, and will positively affect both food preparation and eating. Wooden dining tables and chairs are preferable to glass, metal or marble, and rustic or woven materials would positively enhance a room with a modern high-tech look by soothing its hardness and making it more nurturing.*

▲ *The location of the stove can have a big impact on the quality of your food. The cook should not face directly away from the door, but if it is unavoidable, a shiny, metal toaster or kettle next to the stove – and a windchime near the doorway – will alert him/her to anyone coming into the kitchen. You should avoid having the stove below a window too, because vital energy will be lost through the glass and external wall. Ideally, a triangular arrangement is created with the stove, sink and refrigerator, and as fire is the most natural cooking medium, gas is the first choice for cooking rather than electricity.*

◀ *Although the country cottage look may not be to everyone's taste, it is good to avoid shiny fittings and a lot of harsh metal in your kitchen. They may look clean and bright but they have a more stressful influence on the food. Your aim should be to create an environment in which it is easy to eat without interruption, so you absorb maximum nutrients from your food. Try to avoid placing the table in a busy crossroads, or having too many doors opening onto it; this will make the food difficult to digest. Keep the table away from unsettling cutting energy projected from all sharp corners. Here the flowing lines of these shelves actively enhance the relaxed feel.*

▶ *Good lighting is important. It is always best to work in bright, open spaces so kitchens must be fully illuminated. More localized or focused lighting is better for dining areas. Candles help to create the calm atmosphere necessary for relaxed digestion. Choosing the right colours is vital too. Lighter colours make both rooms more soothing. Greens, yellows and white are good, but tones in the red spectrum can be used effectively in dining areas if you want to stimulate conversation.*

tips for kitchens/dining rooms

- Use natural materials whenever possible: bright, shiny, fast-food kitchens are stressful.

- The stove, sink and refrigerator should form a triangle. Where a sink is next to a stove, put a wooden chopping board between them to maintain the balance between the energies of fire and water.

- Wherever possible, try to introduce smooth lines and curves rather than sharp angles to encourage the chi to flow more evenly around the room.

- Work in bright, open spaces; eat in a calmer, comfortably lit environment.

- No clocks create a timeless and unhurried environment in which to eat.

- Wooden dining tables provide good, solid support and are preferable to sharp-edged glass ones.

▼ *Look at the balance of the shapes in your dining room: circles generate creative ideas and a round table will draw people together and is great for group conversations. The disciplined arrangement of the pictures behind will prompt more practical issues.*

◄ *This quiet corner well out of the way of any kitchen activity will be a good place to relax and wind down. Remember that you can – and should – use paintings to reinforce a mood. Here one of the pictures features an appropriate instruction to slow down.*

If there is light in the soul, there will be beauty in the person.
If there is beauty in the person, there will be harmony in the house.

If there is harmony in the house, there will be order in the nation.
If there is order in the nation, there will be peace in the world.
CHINESE PROVERB

THE HOME OFFICE

Recent advances in international communications and computer technology mean that more and more people are going to be able to work from home. The impact of this revolution on our lives is already here, and will continue to be dramatic, for while working from home can create a real sense of freedom, it also puts at risk the role of your home as the sanctuary to which you retreat at the end of each working day. Indeed, your office could end up taking over your home. You can create a stress-free environment, however, by achieving a balance in how space will be used, and by establishing strong boundaries, so that although you cannot leave the office behind, you can at least shut the door and bring closure at the end of each working day.

It is best to have the room you choose as your home office or study close to your front door; this offers a strong relationship with the outside world, and means that work-related visitors do not intrude in your private one by walking through family rooms.

It is easier to create an uplifting, supportive working environment if a person is based at home than if he/she goes out to work. This large room, with a natural wooden floor, a view out across the garden and a living bay tree in the room itself, is an inspiring place to work – with lots of storage space too. The focal point though, is the square desk, in order that this creativity turns into money.

tips for home offices

• An ordered study will empower you.

• Be organized. Keep the room tidy
  because a messy environment will
  disturb your ability to think clearly.

• Keep the room fresh; remove waste
  daily; do not let stagnation build up.

• Be sure that you can, and do, close
  off your office at the end of each day.

• Make sure everything works; fix
  anything as soon as it breaks down.

• Wherever possible, use natural
  materials in a home office.

• Make sure you position a cleansing
  plant – poinsettia, spider or jade
  plant – beside any electrical units to
  counteract the debilitating electro-
  magnetic discharges, and add an
  ionizer to boost negative ions.

• Square furniture is best for decision-
  making and financial work; curves,
  circles and ovals are better for
  creative thinking.

◀ *Deciding on the position of your desk is very important, as is the arrangement of the space, so that energy can flow easily. Try to have a solid wall behind you rather than a window or open walkway; at least ensure that you have a clear view of the door. Make sure, however, that you are not sitting opposite it – right in the path of the energy coming into the room. It is vital, too, to make sure that there are no sharp angles pointing directly towards you.*

▲ *The squareness and good lighting here will help with concentration whilst there are enough symbols and interesting objects to stimulate the imagination too. A room like this will give a huge boost to a child and will support powerful thinking – a great learning environment for a child.*

Life is a journey not a destination. So is your home.

MOREL FOURMAN

BATHROOMS

The bathroom is a private space where we are in communion with ourselves late at night and first thing in the morning, where we should be able to feel relaxed as we unwind before bed, and squeaky clean and ready to brave anything at the start of a new day. A small bathroom will make you think more intensely about your body: bright lighting and big mirrors will create an illusion of space and encourage you to stretch and expand your horizons.

Bathrooms are for purification and cleansing and therefore should be clean, airy and simple; they need good ventilation and lighting, privacy and minimal clutter. But they also represent waste, and ideally should be kept as far away as possible from the kitchen. Wherever it is, the bathroom must function efficiently because the flow of life-enhancing water is linked symbolically both with personal internal plumbing and the flow of wealth and opportunities; plumbing problems will have a direct impact on both your health and your financial situation.

This room is the ideal place for housing your largest mirror, so if you have the space, think huge – and at most modest, as big as possible. It will encourage you to stretch in the morning and this will expand your energy, which has been contracted while you slept, empowering you for the day ahead.

tips for bathrooms

- Ensure that all the plumbing functions properly – no leaks, or faults with water pressure, or noises. A dripping tap – however slow – can indicate an erosion of your finances.

- Your internal plumbing will reflect the health of your bathroom too. If you do have physical problems, sort them out when you are doing the house's plumbing.

- Avoid triangles, sharp edges and corners, and cold or hard metallic materials. They will make you feel very uncomfortable when you are undressed and feeling vulnerable. Hanging soft towels in the bathroom will help to warm the room and make you feel cosy and secure.

- If the toilet is next to the kitchen, hang a ceramic mobile between the two rooms to moderate the balance of the different energies.

- Mirrored tiles can present real problems because they literally slice up your image, and this can have a very disturbing effect.

▼ *Energy drains away from the bathroom as if magnetically, so try to avoid having your bathroom near the front door, where the chi is most active and has the most force. Nor is 4 Wind or the centre of the home an ideal place for a bathroom, but if it is unavoidable, hang a small convex mirror on the outside of the door to prevent energy going in and being lost, put upright plants around the toilet, and keep the lid down.*

▶ *We use mirrors daily and most often in bathrooms, so it is very important that the image you see is a true reflection. Pay attention to the clarity of the glass and ensure that the mirror is positioned so that you see as much as possible of your reflection and that it is not split. This can affect your health and add to confusion and indecision.*

◀ Tall, upright plants, with their strong upward energy, will counteract the draining effect of the plumbing on the room's energy. Windows, good for bathroom ventilation, can also help by giving a view of the outside world – introducing elements of the natural world – the positive effect magnified here by the reflected mirror image. Yet facing mirrors will create problems too, if your reflection is multiplied into infinity; this orchid once again has a corrective function, acting as a screen to prevent this. Although here the blind can be drawn to enclose the space, it is generally better to position the bath away from the window.

▶ The squareness of the mirror and tiled walls is balanced here by the round basins, lights, shells and boxes. Squares and rectangles represent the human need for order and balance. A happy combination of squares and circles is a metaphor for an equilibrium between Earth and Heaven. Big mirrors expand space in bathrooms which have no outside window; hanging a photograph, painting or something natural opposite will have a similar effect.

Sometimes the most urgent and vital thing you can do is take a complete rest.

ASHLEIGH BRILLIANT

BEDROOMS

Your bedroom is your sanctuary, a nurturing retreat where deep relaxation and rejuvenation are inevitable. Increasingly, people are being subjected to an overload of information, particularly at work, and this causes constant and debilitating stress. At the end of a long and active day, therefore, what you really need is a nurturing haven, which will relax and soothe you, not a place of distraction and stimulation. One of the greatest gifts you can ever give yourself is a bedroom as far away as possible from the noise and stress of the outside world, a quiet sanctuary containing precious little; you really don't want to stimulate the eye or the mind.

A small, symmetrical bedroom is ideal, because the energy is more settling and contained – as long as everything that might affect the quality of your sleep has been removed. All the clothes you have worn during the day which have picked up energies from the world outside should be banished to a separate dressing room or closed storage area.

The white and pale oatmeal colours in this room make it extremely cool and restful. The natural tones – the off-white on the walls and the warm wooden frames of the bed and pictures moderate any starkness. The plain furnishings are a soothing contrast to the collection of flower studies on the wall.

◄ *Where your bedroom is also used as a study it is important to create some boundary between your private time and your work. Don't have unread books and piles of unfinished work in your line of vision just before you go to sleep. Screen off the area around your bed to create a strong boundary and force you to switch off from the day.*

► *Create a sanctuary of your bedroom – make it a place to which you can retreat. Relaxation requires soft, gentle lines and shapes; art and ornament that is sharp, angular or disquieting should be discarded. Use soft cushions, voluminous drapes, flowers or plants and favourite things to bring a sense of calm. It is easier to transform a smaller room into a private retreat because it not only feels cosier, but its size often prevents it from becoming the focus of activity. In a room with sloping ceilings add tall headboards and uplighting to counteract the pressure of the downward energy.*

◀ *Your choice of room should be determined by comfort rather than by size – ideally it should be symmetrical. Corners and nooks work better in living spaces; they make a room busy, whereas a bedroom really needs to be a sanctuary. Colour is a powerful tool, having as much effect on the nature of a room as its shape. Blue is associated with introspection and serenity so it is ideal for a bedroom, though sometimes it can feel cold; here the light wooden floor is warming and the orange flowers add a necessary touch of vibrancy to the otherwise restrained decor.*

▶ *Ceiling beams, an authentic detail in older or country houses, in fact have a very detrimental effect on the quality of your sleep. You can minimize the beams' effect with a canopy; it acts as a protective cover while you sleep and ensures that the energy above you moves smoothly. Historically, people slept in wooden-framed beds which contained their energy as they slept; the long stool here serves the same function, the green adding its balancing and restful properties to soothe the spirit. Rugs would be a happy addition as stone can feel cold in a bedroom.*

▼*A simple and natural environment fosters a corresponding lifestyle. There is a beautiful simplicity and sense of calm in this room where everything is stored away and all materials are natural. Although there is a total absence of soft shapes, the horizontal lines of the bed and door balance perfectly the vertical lines of the door frame and wardrobe. This storage is much better than mirrored door fronts, which are very disturbing to the quality of sleep.*

tips for bedrooms

- Ensure there is nothing to disturb you while you sleep – mirrors, electrical appliances and vibrant colours – denying you total relaxation.

- Position your bed carefully. Give yourself a clear view of the door, and have a solid wall behind you rather than an open area or a window. Try to avoid sleeping directly in line with the door; you will be lying in the path of any energy as it enters the room.

- If your back is to the door, hang a small mirror on the wall opposite, positioned so as to allow you to see anyone entering the room.

- Cover any mirror-fronted wardrobes with a light curtain at night, as mirrors expand the energy of the room then, when it should be settling.

- Metal-framed beds amplify the electro-magnetic radiation from other electrical equipment and wiring in the house; wooden beds are better.

- Always choose natural fabrics for sheets, blankets and pillowcases.

◄ *It is worth noting that bedrooms that look west are preferable for people who find it difficult to settle, while rooms facing the sunrise are ideal for those who find it hard to wake up. Where you want to position your bed is also crucial because you will be spending around one third of your life in it. It is best placed with the head protected by a solid wall behind it, with a good view of the door. Flanking the bed with cloth-covered bedside tables and hanging a tapestry or quilt behind the bed will soften the environment; angular or disquieting pictures should be avoided. This room has good symmetry and pairing, its matching side tables will act as positive reinforcements for a relationship.*

The real voyage of discovery consists not in seeking new landscapes but in having new eyes.

MARCEL PROUST

CHILDREN'S ROOMS

Children's rooms should be simple and cosy, full of symbols representing possibility and imagination; spaces where it will be possible to develop a strong sense of self as well as enjoying the carefreeness of youth.

Children change fast as they grow up, they seem different from month to month, so, obviously, they need their surroundings to reflect this momentum: you should plan to be re-arranging furniture and redecorating at least every two years.

Children will, of course, react as individuals to colours, shapes and images, and you should be receptive, because they seem to know intuitively what is good for them. Keeping in mind some of the basic dos and don'ts that have applied in the rest of the house, you should help them to choose how they want the room to be decorated instead of imposing on them your own desires. Similarly, if you can ensure that the room is kept clean, by providing organized storage, you will encourage the children themselves to keep the room tidily ordered. It is really important to let children personalize their space. Balance is the key: give them the freedom to be creative, but give them security too.

▶ *If a child adjusts where he or she sleeps in a bed or physically moves to another part of the room during the night, you should re-arrange the furniture; if they simply do not sleep well, check that there is nothing under the bed or hanging over it. Here, then, the muslin canopies should be removed, unless they are actually used as mosquito nets, to let energy circulate easily above the beds' inhabitants. Some children might find this mural frightening, but the animals, if perceived as friendly, will be perfect guardians. The children's relationship will be enhanced by the matching beds; the table between is a useful boundary.*

◀ *Organize the space to let your child see the bedroom door from his/her bed, as this will increase their sense of security. Even in a small room, consider hanging a curtain to screen off the bed – the settled space – from the more active, creative play area, to minimize any distractions from sleep's restorative power, and thereby increase your child's energy and vitality. The verticality of the tall cupboards, shelf units and stripes here will lend positive reinforcement to the upward thrust of the child's development.*

▶ *Be careful: in a child's room, supposed to nurture both activity as well as sleep, blue may be too cooling. Particularly if the room is north-facing and gets little light, it could make a child feel introverted. The wall colour and the fabric used here, which combines geometry with animals, and a cool blue with warmer tones, would be good for a child in need of stability and order. The furniture and toys are very structured and reflect a child with an orderly mind.*

◄ *If you provide a fun place for children to hold their treasures, you will encourage them to take care of their belongings and be tidier. This bright structure of red tubing and yellow shelves makes an ideal unit: it offers children easy access and an ordered space in which to store their books and toys. If you create the essential framework, the processes will follow more naturally.*

► *Creativity is stimulated in this play area by the curves of the stools and table; bright, primary colours, as well as being great fun, are generally ideal for such spaces too. Some very active children might find them over-stimulating, so it would be even better if this were a separate playroom and not visible from the sleeping area. Images of animals, providing that they are recognizable and friendly, and dogs particularly, lend reinforcement to the security offered by cuddly toys.*

tips for children's rooms

- Your children should feel that they have some control over how their rooms are decorated; it will be good preparation for the decision-making of later life.

- Make sure the room has a focal point: a mobile by a window, or a special place for certificates. A clock is good, too; its constant presence cultivates a sense of time-keeping.

- If possible, separate children of different ages to let them develop more self-reliance. And allow them privacy to help develop their independence and self-esteem.

- Have a light switch close to the bed so they can control when they want to read without getting out of bed.

- Positioned away from the bed, a full-height mirror will help a child to develop a sense of self.

- Avoid bunk beds: one child will be too close to the ceiling while the other is cramped below.

Where you live is what you become.
Your home mirrors the challenge, opportunities and direction of your life.

GINA LAZENBY

◀ *Amplify the effect of any feng shui placement – here a collection of bright objects – by placing the items with a specific intention in mind. Each time you look at them you will be reminded about what it is that you are aiming to achieve.*

MOVING FORWARD
10 SIMPLE STEPS

1 *Changes come from within*

Any transformation you effect in your subconscious will be reflected in your external world. Deep, long-lasting change can only be achieved when you recognize this and pay attention to your inner bagua. Real harmony at home will only be achieved when you begin to design your life from the inside out.

2 *Be inspired by your home*

Armed with the knowledge of feng shui, you can make your homes into places of personal power. Once you fully accept the notion that your environment is simply a mirror for your life, you should take a good hard look around you and decide if you like what you see. If you don't like it, change it – it really is as simple as that. Then, if you surround yourself with images that relate to your future desires, it will help make them more real and achievable.

3 *Reconnect with nature*

For all the advantages of modern, technological living, we have created a way of life grossly out of step with nature. Many of the lifestyle problems we face today simply did

▶Remember, the more organized your environment, the more organized and structured your lifestyle becomes. As our lives are now more complex, we can ensure that we can cope and therefore reduce stress by having everything sitting reassuringly in its rightful place.

not exist thousands of years ago. Electricity may give us power but when we unknowingly live in its force-field, it also steals our well-being from us. Find out what you can do to ensure that you are living in as natural an environment as possible.

4 Strong personal energy can surmount most environments

The possession of strong personal energy can transcend most environments, however difficult they may seem. Apart from having an indomitable spirit and an iron will in the face of adversity, you can also make a a conscious decision to take control of your physical health, providing

yourself with nourishing food and quality sleep, which will inevitably benefit your mental state. Find out what else you can do to effect those things over which you do have an influence, which will help to overcome those over which you do not.

5 Don't be confused by different systems

You will get all sorts of different advice from different people and different books. They are all aiming for the same goal and are just individual interpretations, so you should look to the source with which you feel most comfortable. As a last resort, when you are not sure what to do, you should ask your home. This may sound strange – cranky even – but a conversation held in a quiet moment or while you meditate will yield all sorts of surprising wisdoms and home truths!

6 Create space for your new life

There is no need to live like a minimalist, but you have to keep things moving, or there will not be enough space in your home or your life to attract anything new. If you introduce mirrors into such a cluttered environment, they will double the size of your problem. Just keep checking that you either love something or use it; if not, give it (or throw it) away.

7 Make the changes slowly and carefully

Take it all step by step, so that you can keep a check on what works and what doesn't. Watch for strange coincidences, like when a plant placed with strong intention for family harmony one day precipitates a phone call from an estranged relative the next morning. Keep on making the changes and observing the results – even if they are not so immediately obvious.

8 Make your home a sanctuary

Whatever it takes, your home needs to be able to restore you – particularly if you feel worn down by the

► *Water in your environment is a powerful symbol of wealth and opportunities flowing into your life. Fish activate its positive potential even more by adding movement to the water. This tank is a wonderful contemplative focus when relaxing in the bath.*

stresses of modern life. Learn more about what elements in your environment actually add to your stress and tension and introduce as many elements as you can that will help to rebalance you. Above all, concentrate on your bedroom and make sure that it really is a calm, nurturing shelter which can and will de-stress you.

9 *Good energy at home supports your work*

Make sure, first of all, that where you live really does support you. Protect your own energy with a good diet so that you will be less affected by electro-magnetic stresses and difficult environments; and create the best possible surroundings for your own work space – whether at home or elsewhere. It is essential that you do whatever you can to make this work area as joyful, natural and uplifting as you can.

10 *Allow energy to move freely*

If your home is set up so that energy can easily move through your front door and has nothing obstructing its flow around the house, you will find your life will open up too. The degree to which you adjust your routines to compensate for awkwardly arranged spaces is reflected in the fact that your life will be a series of compromises. Design a home that speaks love, success, abundance and opportunity throughout its entire structure and you will find that this is how your life will be.

BIBLIOGRAPHY

FOR A FURTHER UNDERSTANDING OF PLACEMENT

- *Feng Shui in 10 Simple Lessons* by Jane Butler-Biggs, Watson-Guptill
- *The Feng Shui House Book* by Gina Lazenby, Watson-Guptill
- *Feng Shui Made Easy* by William Spear, Harper San Francisco
- *Feng Shui Handbook* by Master Lam, Henry Holt
- *The Western Guide to Feng Shui* by Terah Kathryn Collins, Hay House Inc.
- *Interior Design with Feng Shui* by Sarah Rossbach, E. P. Dutton
- *Feng Shui: The Book of Cures* by Nancilee Wydra, NTC/Contemporary Publishing
- *Feng Shui* by Angel Thompson, St. Martin's Press
- *Home Design from the Inside Out* by Robin Lennon, Penguin Arkana USA

FOR UNDERSTANDING THE FIVE ENERGIES

- *The Feng Shui Handbook* by Derek Walters, Thorsons
- *Practical Feng Shui* by Simon Brown, Sterling
- *The Complete Illustrated Guide to Feng Shui* by Lillian Too, Element

FOR PRACTICAL SUPPORT IN CLUTTER CLEARING

- *Simplify Your Life* by Elaine St. James, Hyperion

FOR UNDERSTANDING THE TIME DIMENSION

- *Feng Shui Astrology* by Jon Sandifer, Ballantine
- *Principles of Feng Shui* by Simon Brown, Thorsons
- *The Ki: How to Make Your Dreams Come True* by Takashi Yoshikawa, Trafalgar Square

TOWARDS A MORE NATURAL WAY OF LIVING

- *The New Natural House Book* by David Pearson, Fireside
- *The Natural Year* by Jane Alexander, Avon
- *Home Ecology* by Karen Christensen, Fulcrum
- *Places of the Soul* by Christopher Day, Thorsons

AS WITHIN SO WITHOUT - IMPROVING YOUR HEALTH AND ENERGY

- *Your Face Never Lies* by Michio Kushi, Avery Publishing Group
- *Sugar Blues* by William Dufty, Warner Books Inc.
- *The Self Healing Cookbook* by Kristina Turner, Earthtones Press
- *Food and Healing* by Annemarie Colbin, Ballantine
- *The Macrobiotic Way* by Michio Kushi, Avery Publishing Group
- *Food Governs Your Destiny* by Michio and Aveline Kushi, Kodansha International
- *Psychic Protection* by William Bloom, Fireside

LEARNING MORE ABOUT CLEANSING HOMES AND HARMFUL ENERGIES

- *Healthy Home* by Jill Blake, Watson-Guptill
- *Creating Sacred Space with Feng Shui* by Karen Kingston, Broadway Books
- *Sacred Space* by Denise Linn, Ballantine
- *Safe as Houses* by David Cowan and Rodney Girdlestone, Gill & Macmillan Publishers
- *Holistic Home* by Joanna Trevelyan, Sterling
- *The Healing Home* by Suzy Chiazzari, Trafalgar Square
- *Home Safe Home* by Debra Lynn Dadd, Putnam
- *Spirit of the Home* by Jane Alexander, Watson-Guptill

LEARNING MORE ABOUT ANCIENT WISDOM

- *The I Ching translation* by Richard Wilhelm, Princeton
- *The I Ching translation* by Master Ng, Shambhala
- *The Secret Language of Signs* by Denise Linn, Ballantine
- *The Way of the Wyrd* by Brian Bates, Rider

FENG SHUI NETWORK

For information on feng shui courses; consultations for homes and businesses with professional feng shui practitioners, space clearers and dowsers; speakers; professional training; purchasing these recommended books and others, videos and audio cassettes by mail order, *contact:*

Feng Shui Network International (FSNI)

P. O . Box 2133

London, W1A 1RL

England

Tel: +44 (0) 7000 336474

Fax: +44 (0) 1423 712869

Email: Feng1@aol.com

Website: www.fengshuinet.com

Gina Lazenby can be contacted via the above office.

PICTURE CREDITS

THE PUBLISHER WOULD LIKE TO THANK THE FOLLOWING PHOTOGRAPHERS AND ORGANISATIONS
FOR THEIR KIND PERMISSION TO REPRODUCE THE PHOTOGRAPHS IN THIS BOOK

1 Bill Batten/Conran Octopus;
4 Peter Aaron/Esto; 6-7
Alexander van Berge/Elle
Wonen; 8-9 Marie-Pierre
Morel/Christine Puech/MCM; 11
Jonathan Pilkington/Country
Homes and Interiors/Robert
Harding Syndication; 13
Christian Sarramon; 15 above
Pat O'Hara/Getty Images; 15
below Ted Yarwood (Design
Sharon Mimran); 16 above
Robert Harding Picture Library;
16 below Paul Warchol;
17 above Robert Harding
Picture Library; 17 below Fritz
von der Schulenburg/The
Interior Archive; 18 above
Robert Harding Picture Library;
18 below Simon Upton/The
Interior Archive(Artist Graham
Carr); 19 above The Stock
Market; 19 below Karl Dietrich-
Buhler/Elizabeth Whiting &
Associates; 20 above Jim
Ballard/Getty Images; 20 below
Ianthe Ruthven(Hodgson
House, New Hampshire);
21 above Harold Sund/The
Image Bank; 21 below Wayne
Vincent (Lesley Saddington)/The
Interior Archive; 22 above
Robert Crandall/Planet Earth
Pictures; 22 below Richard

Felber; 23 above Jody Dole/The
Image Bank; 23 below Andre
Martin/MCM; 24-25 Wulf
Brackrock; 26 Bill Batten/Conran
Octopus; 27 Simon
Brown/Conran Octopus; 28 Bill
Batten/Conran Octopus;
29 Paul Ryan/International
Interiors(Design John Saladino);
30 Andreas von
Einseidel/Country Homes &
Interiors/Robert Harding
Syndication; 31 Bill
Batten/Conran Octopus;
32-33 Images Colour Library;
34 left John Hall; 34-35 Paul
Ryan/International
Interiors(Design Kriistina Ratia);
36-37 Bild Der Frau/Camera
Press; 37 right Paul Ryan/
International Interiors(Design
James Gager); 38 Richard
Felber; 39 Tom Leighton/
Country Homes &
Interiors/Robert Harding
Syndication; 40 Bill Batten/
Conran Octopus;
41 Richard Felber; 42 Paul
Ryan/International
Interiors(Design Jack Lenor
Larsen); 43 Pieter Estersohn/
LachaPelle (Representation);
44-45 Tim Ridley/The Image
Bank; 46 left Nadia Mackenzie;

46-47 Bill Batten/Conran
Octopus; 48 Tim Beddow/The
Interior Archive; 49 Gilles de
Chabaneix/Marie Kalt/MCM;
50-51 Chris Meads; 51 right
Simon Upton/The Interior
Archive; 52 Marianne
Majerus/Country Homes &
Interiors/Robert Harding
Syndication; 53 Bill
Batten/Conran Octopus;
54 Paul Ryan/International
Interiors(Design J Balasz); 55
Brigitte/Camera Press; 56-57
Joe Cornish; 58 left Christopher
Simon Sykes/The Interior
Archive; 58-59 Andreas von
Einseidel/Elizabeth Whiting &
Associates; 60-61 Bill Batten/
Conran Octopus;
61 right Bild Der Frau/Camera
Press; 62-63 Hans Wolf/The
Image Bank; 64 Ray Main;
65 Schoner Wohnen/Camera
Press; 66 Joshua Greene; 67
Simon Upton/World of
Interiors(Courtesy of Keith
Skeel); 68-69 Schoner
Wohnen/Camera Press; 69 right
Alexander van Berge;
70-71 Chuck Place/The Image
Bank; 72 Simon Brown/The
Interior Archive; 73 Ted Yarwood
(Design Sharon Mimran); 74 Bill

Batten/Conran Octopus;
75 Bill Batten/Conran Octopus;
76 Simon Brown/The Interior
Archive(Design Clodagh Nolan);
77 Eric Morin; 78 Tim Beddow/
The Interior Archive(Architect
Arthur Duff); 79 Michael
Crockett/Elizabeth Whiting &
Associates; 80-81 Eric Meola/
The Image Bank; 82 Bill Batten/
Conran Octopus; 82-83 Fair
Lady/Camera Press; 84 Schoner
Wohnen/Camera Press;
85 Living/Camera Press;
86 Bild Der Frau/Camera Press;
87 Schoner Wohnen/Camera
Press; 88-89 Images Colour
Library; 90 Deidi von Schwaen;
91 Marie-Pierre Morel/
Catherine Ardouin/MCM;
92-93 Henry Wilson/The
Interior Archive(Design Lionel
Copley)